FLORAL DESIGNS

for

RIBBON EMBROIDERY

Camellias (page 40)

FLORAL DESIGNS

for

RIBBON EMBROIDERY

Joyce Randall

Kangaroo Press

To Madeline
who introduced me to
this fascinating pastime

Reprinted 1993
First published in 1992 by Kangaroo Press Pty Ltd
3 Whitehall Road Kenthurst NSW 2156 Australia
P.O. Box 6125 Dural Delivery Centre NSW 2158
Typeset by G.T. Setters Pty Limited
Printed in Hong Kong by Colorcraft

ISBN 0 86417 431 4

Contents

Introduction

Ribbon embroidery, like many delightful old crafts, is coming back into its own. It provides a medium for the expression of individual ideas in your choice of colours, designs and materials. It is exciting to experiment with the wonderful range of coloured ribbons available to the embroiderer—silk, satin, velvet, rayon and polyester—and to combine them with some of today's beautiful embroidery threads. There is almost a freestyle element to ribbon embroidery—you can closely follow the designs in this book, for example, or use them as a basis for your own designs.

The designs in this book use only a few basic stitches and techniques, but do not feel constrained by this. You can use any kind of stitch you need to achieve the effect you want.

Although most of the designs have been worked as framed pictures, they can be adapted for use on blouses, cushions, vests, shawls, soft slippers or slip-on sandals, evening bags, small purses, belts—the list is long. They can be repeated or reversed for panels and borders on dresses. Parts of some designs could be picked out for small articles such as pincushions or embroidered brooches.

Materials

Fine fabrics like silk or crinkled polyester are excellent as backgrounds for the fine silk or polyester ribbons which are used for really delicate work. They are best for beginners as the silk ribbon pulls through more easily.

Firm fabrics like linen, cotton, velvet and velveteen are especially suitable for use with satin ribbon or wider ribbons, as they do not tear easily and will stand up to thicker ribbon being pulled through. Hand knitted or loosely woven woollen fabrics can take wider ribbon, but always test your chosen fabric before working it. Ribbons too wide or too thick can tear fine fabrics.

For more robust and colourful work, and for larger flowers and designs, satin ribbon from 2 mm to 15 mm is good. Nylon taffeta ribbon can be a little wider still.

Transferring designs

To transfer a traced design to the fabric, pin the design in place and slip a piece of graphite paper (obtainable at art shops), shiny side down, between design and fabric. Pin this in place also, to prevent rubbing on the fabric. Use a fine pointed biro to go over the design. This is best done on a hard surface. If using a frame, position the fabric in the frame first as it is difficult to get in position after the tracing is done, and smudging may occur. Find the smooth lid of a jar, or something similar, that can be placed underneath. Afterwards, if necessary, deepen outlines slightly with pencil, but don't make them too dark and obvious.

Alternatively, trace the design onto paper, then pierce holes in the paper with a stiletto or fine sharp skewer at centres and petal tips of the main flowers. With a fadeable pen mark these points on the fabric through the holes. Use a white pencil on coloured materials. Embroider these design elements first, as the penwork fades in two hours. Do the same with the second most important flowers, and so on.

If you want to make up your own floral designs follow a similar procedure. Mark the positions of three main flowers, usually the largest, and complete these first, as often they take up more room than expected. Using the fadeable pen try marking secondary flowers and when satisfied work these too. Do the same with leaves and then mark in stems to make the design flow. To fill out the design, use French knots to represent tiny flowers. Remember uneven numbers of each flower usually look better.

Needles

Chenille needles are essential for ribbon embroidery. Their eyes are large enough for ribbons, and they come in different thicknesses. The finer needles are best for silk ribbon, the thicker ones for satin and wider nylons. Use crewel needles for embroidery cottons.

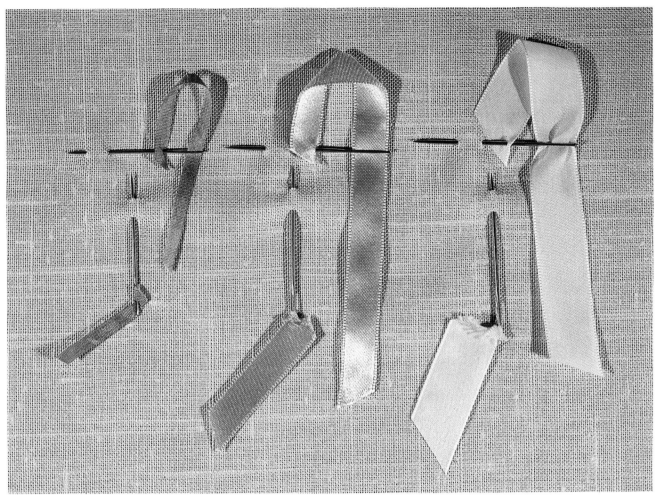

Threading the needle: The top row shows diagonally cut silk, satin and nylon taffeta ribbons with point threaded through needle and the needle taken back through the ribbon near the tip. The second row shows needles ready for sewing.

Threading the needle

When working with silk ribbon, do not use lengths of more than about 22 cm, as the ribbon can fray at the edges before a longer length is used up. Pulling the ribbon through the fabric slowly helps prevent fraying.

Cut across the end of the ribbon diagonally before threading it. Push the pointed tip of the ribbon through the eye of the needle and pull about 2 cm through. Then push the point of the needle back through the ribbon, about 5 mm from the pointed tip. Pull the ribbon back through the needle so that not much more than the tip of the ribbon is left attached. This presents less bulk when pulling the ribbon through the material.

When using satin ribbon or wide nylon ribbon it is of great importance to lessen the obstruction caused when the ribbon reaches the hole in the fabric. To help overcome this push the point of the needle back through the ribbon 5 mm from the tip and close to the selvedge. The ribbon is stronger here. Pull the ribbon back through the needle and twist it backwards and forwards until not much more than the tip is attached. Use the stiletto to gently enlarge the hole if necessary. I find pliers handy sometimes to pull the needle through but I use them only if I think the fabric can take it and when the bulk of the ribbon has been minimised as far as possible.

Starting off

When starting off leave 15 or 20 mm of ribbon at the back of the work. If fine silk or rayon is being used, the next stitch through to the back will often pierce the starting-off end and save finishing off. Do not do this with thicker ribbon as it does not pass through itself easily.

Finishing off

Take the ribbon through to the back and cut off about 2 cm from work. You will probably have several cut-off pieces which will all need securing with needle and thread to stitches at the back of the embroidery. It is nearly impossible to keep the back of the work tidy.

Stitches

Much floral work can be accomplished using plain straight stitches and keeping the ribbon flat. A variation on this is to put the needle through the ribbon when taking it through to the back.

French knots are useful as small flowers to fill out a design. Use silk ribbon or 2–3 mm satin ribbon and bring it through to the right side. Take the ribbon over the tip of the needle and around it once before pushing it through the material close to where it came out—*not* through the same hole or the knot will go through to the back. Keep your thumb over the knot and pull through carefully.

Fly stitches in embroidery thread can be used to fill out a design which might otherwise look a little too open.

Embroider most stems in stem stitch; backstitch can be used for an attractive alternative. For a thicker stem these stitches can be 'whipped' by sewing a thread through each stitch afterwards.

Fly stitch and ribbon roses

Fly stitch on its own is useful to fill out a design. It can also be used to make a base for a small rose. Start with a fly stitch, then bring the thread up again to one side and take it under the centre of the fly stitch to form five spokes of a wheel. Bring the silk ribbon up close to the centre and weave it over and under the spokes until they are covered. Take the ribbon through to the back to finish off.

Always use matching cotton for the wheel spokes. Thick embroidery thread may be used instead of ribbon to fill the roses.

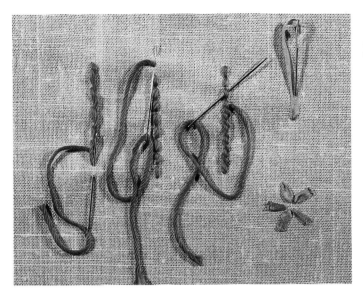

The stitches shown here are, from left to right: stem stitch, back stitch and whipping, all in the dark colour. Taking the needle through the ribbon to the back, and a daisy using this method, are shown in pink.

The top row shows detached chain stitch worked in pink ribbon. The needle goes back through the same hole. The look can be varied by using different length stitches to end up.

The second row shows French knots in a fine blue ribbon. Bring ribbon through to right side of fabric, take it over tip of needle and around it once before pushing needle back through fabric. Do not take it back through the hole it came from, for the knot can easily slip through to the back.

The third row, using mushroom ribbon, shows twisted detached chain stitch. The needle goes back over the ribbon and into a different hole. This stitch can also be ended with different length stitches, like detached chain.

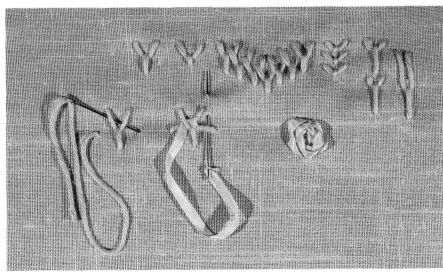

Different ways of working fly stitch are shown in the top row. The second row shows how to make a ribbon rose on a 5-spoked wheel made by starting with a fly stitch. Bring ribbon up next to centre and work it over and under spokes until spokes cannot be seen. Finish off.

Folded roses

Folded roses can be used in designs for really pretty floral effect. Satin ribbon is the best choice. Two designs, Nos 13 and 18, include folded roses made with 7 mm ribbon.

Take a length of ribbon and hold it vertically, folding over horizontally to the right about 14 cm up. Holding with the thumb, take the long end and fold across horizontally to the left. Bring the short end up, followed by the long end across to the right, then short end down and so on until short end of ribbon is used up. Hold the end firmly with the thumb and first finger against the long piece of ribbon and let the folded part go. Still holding on pull the long ribbon back carefully until the rose forms. Secure with a stitch down the middle using matching coloured cotton, and a couple of stitches at the base. Trim ends and sew on to the design where indicated.

Making a folded rose (top row). Long end of ribbon to right, short end down. Then long end to left followed by short end up. Long end to right and short end down, and so on until short end is used up.

Hold the short end firmly against the long piece of ribbon and let folded part go.

The rose forms when the long end is pulled back carefully. Secure with a stitch down the centre, using same coloured cotton, and a couple of stitches at base.

Frames and hoops

The coloured plastic picture frames used for many of the illustrations here are wonderful for beginners and very easy to use. The two sizes used for these designs are: small, 7.5 × 10 cm, and large, 11.5 × 15.5 cm. Each frame comes with an insert, over which the fabric is placed. The insert slips into the frame, keeping the fabric taut while it is being embroidered. Trim fabric off leaving about 4–5 cm all around. (In effect, each picture frame is its own embroidery hoop.)

A wooden embroidery hoop is good for larger designs as it can be moved around. A hoop was used for the blouse designs.

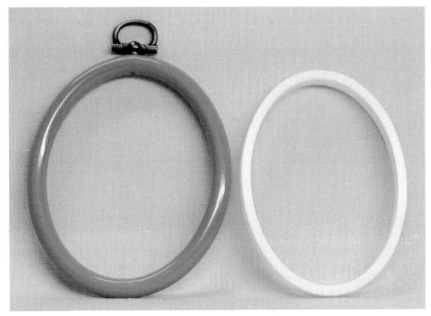

Plastic frame and insert

Back of large frame before glueing on felt to finish off

Finishing off a framed embroidery

You will need:
   A piece of strong cardboard cut to fit inside the frame insert
   A piece of plastic foam sponge the same size, 4–8 mm thick
   Cotton wool
   Double thickness of white lawn or cotton fabric
   A piece of felt to cover back

(Continued on page 14)

Turn the framed embroidery face down. Trim the fabric at the back, leaving 3 cm all the way around. Run a double thread of sewing cotton around the fabric, about 1.5 cm from the raw edge. Do not finish off.

Cut the cotton fabric 5 mm larger than the inside measurement of the insert. (This is used to prevent the colour of the plastic foam showing through the work.) Place the cotton fabric against the back of the embroidery. Over this put the plastic foam layer, then a layer of cotton wool, followed by the cardboard.

Hold the cardboard down while tightly drawing in the gathering thread around the raw edge of the embroidered fabric. Use a couple of stitches to keep the gathering thread in place. Thread the needle again with a double thread and zigzag across the back of the frame, working from side to side and end to end. Pull together as tightly as possible, and finish off. Check to feel that the cardboard is positioned level with the edge of the insert. Cut an oval piece of felt the size of the outer frame, apply craft glue around the edge and stick to back of frame.

The surface of the picture can be protected with Scotchguard if you wish.

The designs

1. Apricot flowers on white blouse

Ribbon 9 mm polyester in apricot and 7 mm in light bright green

Using straight stitches work flowers that are behind others first. Make centres with French knots in thick gold embroidery cotton. Work buds, then put in stems with two strands of stranded green cotton in backstitch. Lastly put in leaves. Finish off back by sewing ends of ribbon down.

(The original was worked on a simple scoop-necked blouse of crinkled polyester.)

2 Roses and gold daises

Frame   7.5 × 10 cm

Fabric   Crinkled polyester

Ribbon   3 mm silk or polyester in mushroom, two pinks, yellow, green and blue

Make ribbon roses first, using fly stitch spokes for a base in matching cotton and weaving the ribbon over and under the spokes. Use straight stitches with needle taken through ribbon to the back for gold daisies. Straight stitches are used for leaves and tiny daisy centres. Backstitch the stems with two strands of cotton. Finish with blue French knots.

Instructions for facing page
Very loose straight stitches are used for the flowers. With a single strand of cotton and tiny stitches catch where necessary to shape them. For stamens use long stitch in three strands of stranded cotton, with two very short stitches side by side at tips. Stems are backstitched with rayon crochet silk or three strands of stranded cotton and then whipped (taking the cotton through the stitches you have already made to make a thicker stem). Work the leaves, then sew ends of ribbon down to finish the back off.

3 Pink azaleas

Frame 11.5 × 15.5 cm

Fabric Fine linen

Ribbon 15 mm polyester in
          pink and 9 mm in green

4 Forget-me-nots

Frame   7.5 × 10 cm

Fabric   Crinkled polyester

Ribbon   3 mm silk or polyester in two blues, green and gold

Work petals with small loose stitches, allowing the petals to stand up a little. For each centre use a short stitch in gold ribbon. Backstitch stems with two strands of green stranded cotton. Leaves are straight stitches with two overlapping at the base.

5 Cream single roses and small pink flowers

Frame 7.5 × 10.5 cm

Fabric Crinkled polyester

Ribbon 7 mm silk or polyester in cream and 3 mm silk or polyester in two pinks, light green and brown

Work cream single rose petals with loose straight stitches. Slip a wooden skewer under the ribbon near the outer edge while pulling it carefully through to the back. This will keep petals wider at the outer edge. For the small pink flowers use loose straight stitches; put a short stitch in each centre using green ribbon. Do the same in the rose centres, surrounding each centre with tiny stitches using two strands of orange stranded cotton. Work these stitches on top of the inner part of the petals to make them more puffy towards the outer edge. Rose leaves are done in brown, taking the needle through the ribbon to the back. Use two strands of stranded cotton for the pale green leaves and stems.

6 Pink daisies and other flowers

Frame   7.5 × 10 cm

Fabric   Crinkled polyester

Ribbon   3 mm silk or polyester in two pinks, pale blue and two greens

Work overlapping straight stitches for the pink daisies with satin-stitched centres in pale green silk. Deep pink flowers are in detached chain, with the darker green ribbon used for leaves and backstitched stems. Other leaves and backstitched stems are in pale green ribbon. Blue French knots have stems of two strands of green stranded cotton.

Instructions for facing page

For the flower petals, straight stitches, left very loose, are used. To keep the petals wide at the outer edge keep a wooden meat skewer handy and slip it under the ribbon near the outer edge while pulling the ribbon carefully through to the back. The centres are composed of a short piece of pale green ribbon folded under at the ends and held in place with tiny stitches. Use six strands of golden yellow stranded cotton to make French knots around the edges of the centres, which should extend over bases of petals, flattening them a little and making them more puffy towards the outer edges. Place one French knot in the middle of each centre. Make leaves with very loose straight stitches; gather them slightly when backstitching the veins. Stems are backstitched also.

7 Pink single roses

Frame   11.5 × 15.5 cm

Fabric   Fine linen

Ribbon   15 mm satin in pink, dark green and light green

8 Red and pink daisies

Frame 7.5 × 10 cm

Fabric Fine linen

Ribbon 3 mm satin in pink, dark red and green

Work daisies in pink and dark red with straight stitches. Use yellow stranded cotton in satin stitch for centres. Leaves are made with overlapping straight stitches in green ribbon. Four strands of matching stranded cotton are used in the backstitched flower stems.

Instructions for facing page
The wide nylon ribbon slips through the crushed polyester fabric with very little trouble. The stitches are mostly straight and *very* loose, requiring tiny stitches in matching colours to shape the flowers. Put the leaves in before backstitching the stems with three strands of stranded cotton or rayon crochet silk.

9 Sweet peas

Frame   13.5 × 13.5 cm

Fabric   Crinkled polyester

Ribbon   15 mm nylon in two pinks and a blue;
9 mm nylon in green

10 White azaleas on blouse

Ribbon   15 mm white polyester; 7 mm green for leaves

Use a fine, sharp wooden skewer to punch holes at the ends of the petals on the traced paper design. Position design on blouse and use a white pencil to make marks through the skewer holes. Straight stitches in white for the flowers are kept very loose and caught where necessary with one strand of cotton and tiny stitches to shape. Leaves are made with straight stitches. Stems are backstitched with rayon crochet silk, or three strands of

stranded cotton, and whipped. For stamens long stitches in pale green crochet silk are used, with two short stitches side by side at tips. Sew ends of ribbon down to finish back off.

(The original design is embroidered on a simple scoop-necked blouse of crinkled polyester.)

11 Yellow and apricot roses

Frame 7.5 × 10 cm

Fabric Crinkled polyester

Ribbon 3 mm silk or polyester in yellow, apricot, brown, mauve and blue

Make roses first, using fly stitch spokes for a base in matching cotton and weaving the ribbon over and under the spokes. Use straight stitches for violets, with tiny French knots in centres made with one single strand of yellow stranded cotton taken over and around the needle once. For brown leaves take needle through the ribbon at the tip of the leaf and pull carefully through to the back. Stems are backstitched with two strands of cotton. The French knots are made last.

Instructions for facing page
Use straight stitches for the petals of the flowers and also for the leaves. Centres are worked with stranded cotton in satin stitch. For the veins in the leaves use long stitches in stranded cotton; backstitch the stems.

12 Yellow daisies

Frame   11.5 × 15.5 cm

Fabric   Fine linen

Ribbon   7 mm satin in yellow and green

13 Pink and blue folded roses with yellow daisies

Frame   11.5 × 15.5 cm

Fabric   Fine linen

Ribbon   7 mm satin in two pinks and a blue; 3 mm satin in yellow, blue and green

14 Pink flowers with violets

Frame   7.5 × 10 cm

Fabric   Fine linen

Ribbon   10 mm satin in pink and 3 mm satin in pale pink, green and mauve

Large pink flowers are worked in straight loose stitches with satin-stitched centres in yellow embroidery cotton. Use straight stitches for violets, with a single tiny stitch in embroidery cotton for centres. Stems are backstitched in satin ribbon and three strands of cotton. Do French knots last.

Instructions for facing page
Make the pink and blue folded roses first and sew in place on design. Use straight stitches for daisies and leaves. Backstitch stems in two strands of cotton or rayon crochet silk (as shown here) and make French knots last.

15 Stephanotis and small red flowers

Frame   11.5 × 15.5 cm

Fabric   Fine linen

Ribbon   7 mm white and green satin and 3 mm red silk or polyester

16 Pink single roses and daisies with French knots

Frame 7.5 × 10 cm

Fabric Silk

Ribbon 7 mm silk or polyester in pink and 3 mm silk or polyester in green, dark red and blue

Work single roses with loose straight stitches. A thin wooden skewer can be used to slip under the ribbon at the outer end of each petal while pulling the ribbon through to the back. This keeps the petals wide at the outer edge. Use detached chain for the daisies with embroidery cotton stitches in centres. Work rose leaves in straight stitches. Backstitch stems with two strands of green cotton and do the French knots. Work rose centres with one tiny stitch in green surrounded by dots in yellow cotton.

Instructions for facing page

Work the white stephanotis in straight stitches with small stitches in green in centres. Small red flowers are done with short, loose straight stitches; yellow embroidery cotton is used to make small single straight stitches in their centres. Pale green leaves have one straight stitch on top of another going through the same holes in the fabric. Ribbons are then pulled sideways and tiny stitches used to hold them in place. Backstitch stephanotis stems with rayon crochet silk or four strands of stranded cotton. Use two strands of stranded cotton for stems and leaves of red flowers.

17 Roses and blue violets

Frame   7.5 × 10 cm

Fabric   Crinkled polyester

Ribbon   3 mm silk or polyester in mushroom, pink, dark blue, green and pale blue

Make the pink and mushroom coloured roses first, using fly stitch in matching cottons as a base and weaving the ribbon over and under the spokes. The violets are worked in dark blue, in straight stitches with a tiny stitch in embroidery cotton in the centre. Straight stitches are used for leaves. Backstitch the stems using two strands of stranded cotton. Finish with French knots in the pale blue ribbon.

Instructions for facing page
Make folded roses first in the purple and darker pink ribbon; stitch in place on design. Use straight short stitches for the pale pink flowers, with two short stitches in centre using two strands of cotton. Rose leaves are also formed with straight stitches. Sew stems with two strands of green stranded cotton and then work French knots in blue ribbon.

18 Pink and purple folded roses with pale pink and blue flowers

Frame   11.5 × 15 cm

Fabric   Fine linen

Ribbon   7 mm satin in purple and two pinks, 3 mm satin in green and 2 mm satin in blue

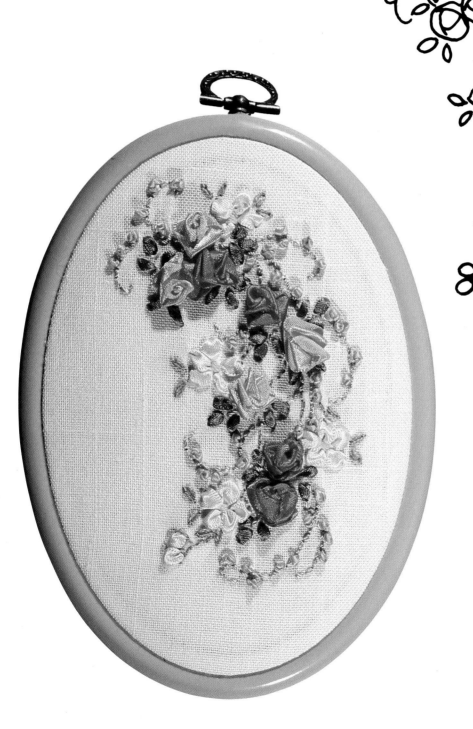

19 Geraniums

Frame 11.5 ✗ 15.5 cm

Fabric Fine linen

Ribbon 10 mm satin in coral and green

20 Pink single roses and other flowers

Frame   7.5 × 10 cm

Fabric   Crinkled polyester

Ribbon   7 mm silk in pink; 3 mm silk or polyester in dark red, dark pink and two greens

Work single roses first in 7 mm pink silk ribbon using loose straight stitches. For each centre use a tiny stitch in dark green ribbon surrounded by gold dots made with single small stitches in embroidery cotton. These are partly on the petals, holding down the silk ribbon towards the centre, thus making petals more puffy towards the outer edge. Red daisies are made with straight stitches with needle taken through ribbon to the back. Use yellow embroidery cotton for centres. Dark pink sprays are worked in detached chain with leaves in straight stitches. Backstitch stems with two strands of green stranded cotton.

Instructions for facing page
Use very loose stitches for flower petals so they can be pulled into shape with tiny stitches in one strand of matching cotton. Leaves are formed by two pieces of ribbon caught down with tiny stitches in the same colour. Stems have been backstitched and whipped in green rayon crochet silk.

21 Blue daisies and violets

Frame 7.5 × 10 cm

Fabric Crinkled polyester

Ribbon 3 mm silk or polyester ribbon in pale blue, violet blue, pink, yellow and green

Use overlapping straight stitches for pale blue daisies with straight stitches in yellow for centres. Work violets in straight stitches, with tiny French knots made with a single strand of cotton taken around the needle once for their centres. For the leaves use detached chain stitches; use the same ribbon to backstitch daisy stems. The other stems are worked in two strands of green stranded cotton. Make pink French knots last.

Instructions for facing page

Work daisies in yellow in detached twisted chain stitch, with green satin stitch embroidery cotton centres. For apricot flowers use detached chain stitch, with straight stitches for leaves. Mauve flowers have two straight stitches to each petal with yellow French knots in centres.

Make blue French knots, then work stems in a single thread of green stranded cotton. Use two strands for the stems and leaves of the mauve flowers. Stems for daisies and apricot flowers are backstitched in green silk ribbon.

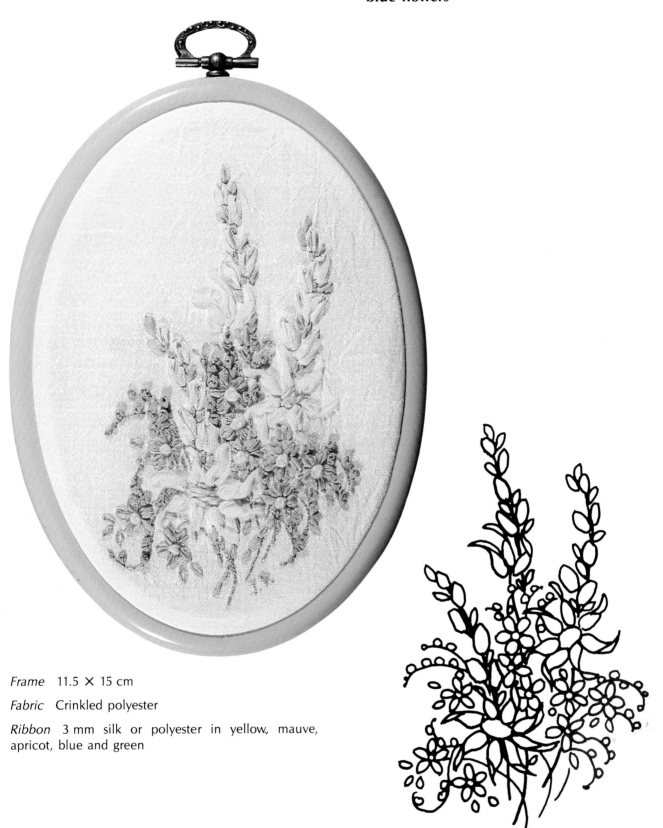

22 Yellow daisies with apricot, mauve and blue flowers

Frame 11.5 × 15 cm

Fabric Crinkled polyester

Ribbon 3 mm silk or polyester in yellow, mauve, apricot, blue and green

23 Camellias

Frame 11.5 cm circular

Fabric Fine linen

Ribbon 15 mm satin in pale pink and dark green

24 Mauve flowers and violets

Frame   7.5 × 10 cm

Fabric   Fine linen

Ribbon   7 mm mauve nylon taffeta; 3 mm satin in violet, green and pink

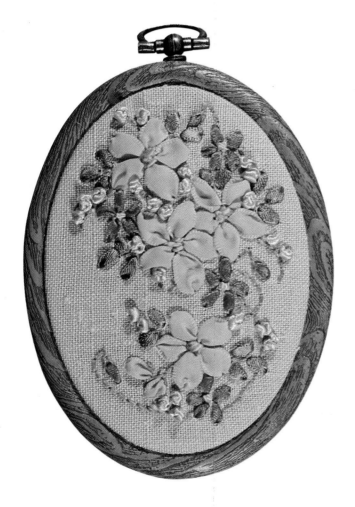

Large mauve flowers are worked in straight loose stitches with two or three short stitches in embroidery cotton for centres. Work violets with straight stitches and make a single stitch in the centre of each with embroidery cotton. Stems are backstitched with two strands of green cotton. Work French knots in pink.

Instructions for facing page
Use very loose stitches for flowers to allow for shaping with tiny stitches in a matching colour. Leaves are left loose also, to permit gathering when backstitching veins. Four strands of matching stranded cotton were used for this, as well as for backstitched stems. Centres were made using short stitches in green with yellow tips in embroidery cotton.

25 Mixed daisies

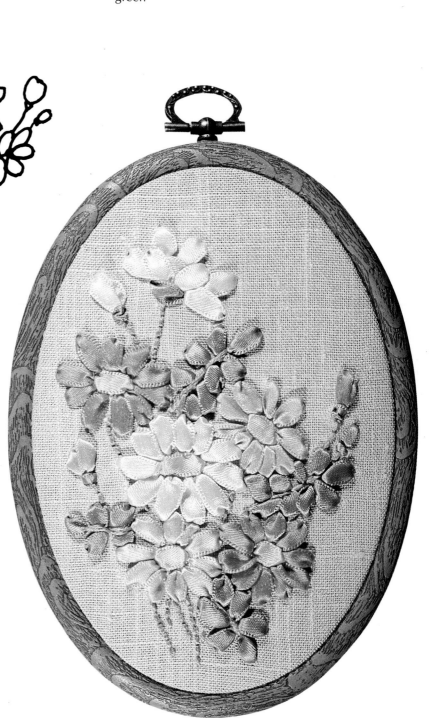

Frame 11.5 × 15.5 cm

Fabric Fine linen

Ribbon 7 mm satin in old gold, peach, yellow, ivory and green

26 Mushroom roses and white daisies

Frame   7.5 × 10 cm

Fabric   Crinkled polyester

Ribbon   3 mm silk or polyester in mushroom, white, two greens and pale blue

Make roses first, using fly stitch spokes for a base in matching cotton and weaving the ribbon over and under the spokes. Use straight stitches with needle taken through ribbon to the back for white daisies. Leaves are also made with straight stitches with the needle passing through ribbon to the back. Do not pull too hard or the tip will go through as well. Use three strands of yellow stranded cotton for daisy centres. Backstitch stems in green cotton and work French knots in pale blue ribbon.

Instructions for facing page

Use straight stitches for the flower petals and leaves. Flower centres are formed with one stitch in golden yellow which needs catching down in places with one strand of matching cotton. For the veins in the leaves use long stitches in matching stranded cotton. Backstitch the stems in the same thread.

27 Folded roses on blue blouse

Ribbon   3 mm silk or polyester in pink, mushroom, blue and purple

Use a fine wooden skewer to punch holes through rose centres on the tracing paper. Place paper in position on blouse and use a white pencil to make marks through holes on to the blouse. Start with a fly stitch the size of the diameter of the rose, bringing the thread up again and taking it under the centre of the fly stitch to form five spokes of a wheel. Bring the silk ribbon up close to the centre and weave it over and under the spokes until they are covered. Take the ribbon through to the back to finish off. Always use matching cotton for the wheel spokes. (Instead of ribbon, thick embroidery thread may be used for the roses.)

Punch holes in tips and bases of leaves and use white pencil as before. Sew leaves in twisted chain stitch using purple ribbon. Stems can be marked freehand with white pencil, or use holes in paper as before.

(The original was worked on a simple round-necked blouse of crinkled polyester.)

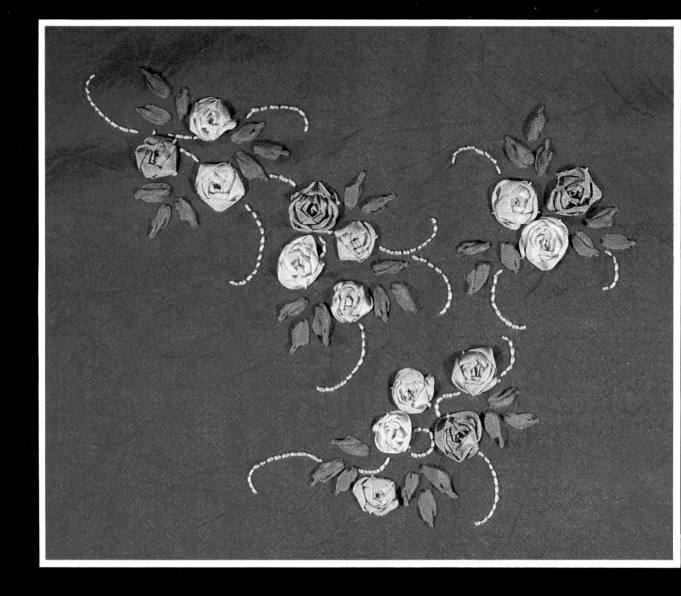

28 Jasmine

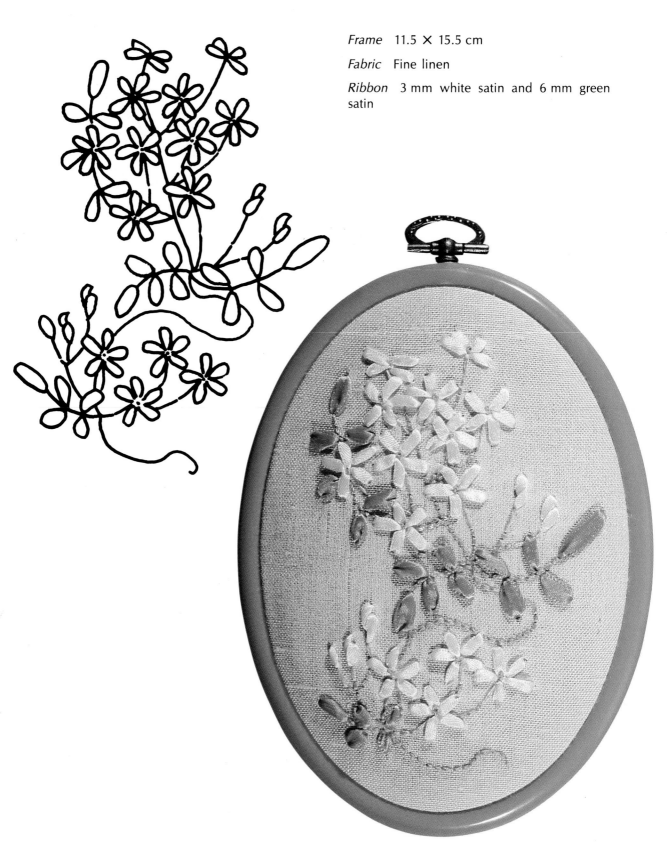

Frame 11.5 × 15.5 cm

Fabric Fine linen

Ribbon 3 mm white satin and 6 mm green satin

29 Wisteria

Frame   7.5 × 10cm

Fabric   Fine linen

Ribbon   7 mm satin in mauve and 3 mm satin in green and purple

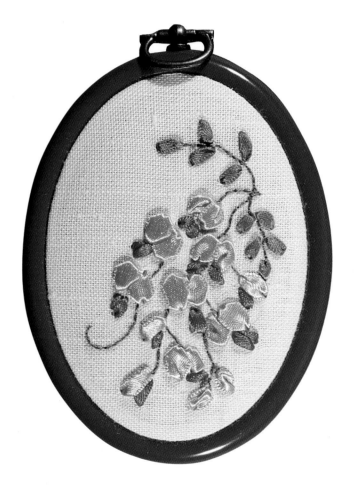

Work flowers and leaves with straight stitches. Use two strands of stranded cotton to backstitch stems.

Instructions for facing page
Work flowers first with straight stitches. French knots in the centres are made with one strand of stranded cotton taken around the needle once. Backstitch stems with two strands of stranded cotton; for the pink part of the stems use two strands of pink to make one long stitch. Make the leaves and finish off the back.